meet Mr. Prduct

meet mr. Product

The Art of the Advertising Character

WARREN DOTZ • MASUD HUSAIN

CHRONICLE BOOKS
SAN FRANCISCO

Sambo • c. 1972
Sambo's restaurants
Detail of restaurant menu

Library of Congress Cataloging-in-Publication Data available.

ISBN 978-0-8118-3589-3

Manufactured in China.

Art direction: Masud Husain and Warren Dotz
Cover and book design: Masud Husain

10 9 8 7 6

Chronicle Books LLC
680 Second Street
San Francisco, California 94107

www.chroniclebooks.com

Cover and pages 2 – 3:
Mr. Milkman • c. 1959
Dairy Product Advertising Company
Detail of promotional store display

8 INTRODUCTION

INTRODUCTION

CHIQUITA, TONY, AND ELSIE—RECOGNIZE THESE NAMES? THEY REPRESENT SOME OF THE BEST-LOVED AD CELEBRITIES OF THE TWENTIETH CENTURY. Although many ad characters have had short-lived careers, others have been around for a hundred years or more. Enticing consumers to buy products from frozen vegetables to packaged cake mix, from fast-food burgers to automobile tires, these imaginatively conceived and illustrated product "spokes-characters" personify the businesses they represent. Many of these businesses began small, but a good number grew to dominate their fields—in large part due to their famous icons.

Advertising characters got their start just before the turn of the twentieth century. Rarely in American history has the population grown so fast. This tremendous growth, largely attributable to the emigration from Europe and Asia, resulted in an expanding labor force and new consumer markets. Manufacturing inventions and innovations led to efficient mass production and packaging of consumer products. Railroads could now transport manufacturers' merchandise to all cities between the Atlantic and Pacific coasts rapidly and cheaply. The expansion of wage-earning jobs allowed less time for people to make staple foods for themselves, thus necessities were transformed into consumables. As individually packaged goods replaced the sacks and barrels of bulk merchandise, manufacturers found new signboards—the wrappers, boxes, and labels—on which to promote their products.

Significant changes in the media also occurred. Magazines as we know them today were really born in the last three decades of the nineteenth century. With the means to produce and distribute them nationally, a new breed of publisher came forth to create periodicals of entertainment, popular fiction, and advice. The five-cent magazine arrived in the form of *Harper's*, the *Ladies' Home Journal*, and

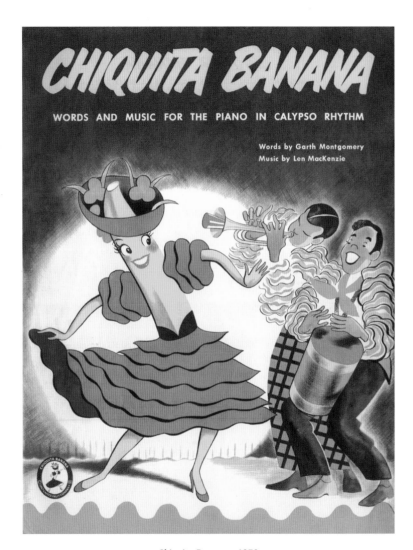

Chiquita Banana • 1950
Chiquita bananas
Cover of promotional sheet music

Better Homes and Gardens, to name a few. Magazines provided a powerful new avenue for marketing—advertising that could easily spread the word about a manufacturer's product all over the country. The amount of advertising that magazines carried was comparable to modern magazine advertising, with literally scores of pages filled with colorful, enticing illustrations and creative sales prose.

The makers of patent medicine pioneered the early merchandising of packaged, labeled goods in the 1800s. For thousands of wounded men returning to their homes after the Civil War, bottled patent medicine was the only kind of medical aid available. As a result, patent medicine advertising dominated the media toward the end of the nineteenth century. Their often fraudulent claims gave rise to the Pure Food and Drug Act of 1906, the first federal law to protect the health of the public and the first to control advertising.

As manufacturers became aware that their containers and products needed to be both distinctive and readily identifiable, names and designs evolved out of commonly recognized symbols and everyday figures. Before advertising and consumer psychology developed into fields of their own, almost 75 years later, these early trademarks were usually created by someone at the manufacturing company trying to encapsulate their product in what seemed to be an appropriate symbol. Most of the earliest advertising characters—like the Arm and Hammer symbol of the flexing bicep, the John Deere Company's leaping deer, and the Durham Tobacco bull—were less characters in the modern sense than very simple trademarks designed to indicate the maker of a product. As they were initially competing against unlabeled and non-trademarked bulk merchandise, these symbols needed to simply distinguish themselves by being decorative, recognizable, and culturally popular. The Arm and Hammer (1867) trademark plays off of mythology, connoting the Roman god Vulcan, the god of fire and metalworking. The original owner of this company previously owned the Vulcan Spice Mills and used the same mark even though it did not have much to do with baking soda and spices. The owner of Durham tobacco appropriated the image of a bull (1860s) from an English mustard. The deer logo for John Deere (1873), obviously, is a simple play on the inventor's name.

Aunt Jemima • c. 1946
Aunt Jemima's pancake mix
Cover of promotional recipe booklet

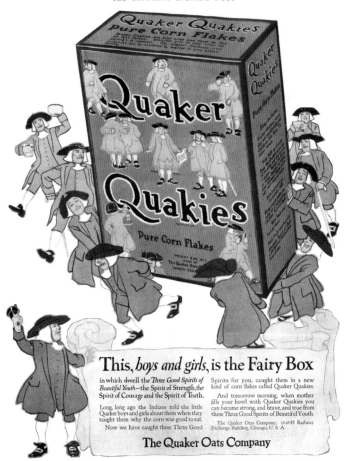

Quaker Oats Man • 1920
Quaker Quakies cereal
Magazine ad

Some clever merchandisers realized that increased promotion would sell more products, which in turn, would accelerate recognition of their advertising trademark by the public. The Quaker Oats Company was particularly good at this. The company's initial trademark in 1877 was a lean and austere Quaker holding a scroll that displayed the word "Pure"—a serviceable equation as Quakers were admired for their thrift and integrity. The owner of Quaker Oats, Henry Crowell, was an enthusiastic advertiser, pioneering the use of four-color illustrated cartons, individually packaged samples, market testing, extensive magazine advertising, and promotional contests among other marketing techniques and approaches. Consumers were asked to cut out the Quaker figure and mail it to the company, which offered attractive premiums to those who did, and this program further impressed the trademark upon the public. By 1893, the company realized that the gaunt and serious trademark Quaker was not as consumer friendly as he could be, so they transformed him into a genial, plump, and rosy-cheeked fellow, similar to the one we know today.

Advertising spokes-characters such as this had the effect of bringing larger companies down to human scale. In a time of public uprootedness and migration, these early smiling and gesturing "Mr. Products" served as a reassuring presence, a comforting substitute for the familiar face of a local merchant. Far from being complex, early advertising spokes-characters simply and literally embodied the chief characteristic of their products—whether it was purity, strength, gentleness, naturalness, or low cost. Thus the Bon Ami chick promoted the cleanser's gentle "scratchless" quality, the Argo corn starch Indian Maiden epitomized nature's healthful bounty, and Aunt Jemima conveyed the promise of delicious and wholesome Southern cooking.

As early modern-day advertising became slightly more sophisticated, characters were developed to specifically emphasize their products' unique selling proposition in relation to their competitors. This led to characters such as the Morton Salt Girl who, with the jingle "When It Rains, It Pours!," reinforced the message that only Morton Salt wouldn't become sticky during humid weather. The Uneeda Biscuit Boy, clad in a yellow rain slicker, symbolized how fresh a prepackaged soda cracker could be, shielded from the elements in a "sanitary, waxed, air-and-moisture proof package." And the Michelin Man, known as Bibendum or "Bib" (the Latin word *bibendum*, means "to drink"), emphasized the ability of the French company's air-filled tires to outperform solid ones by "drinking up" all obstacles on the road. Modern-day advertising agencies continue to use this strategy of highlighting the most relevant idea in a product category. Contemporary ad icons like the Maytag repairman and Morris the Cat, have been around for decades: the Maytag repairman is "the loneliest man in town" because of the dependability of the company's washers and dryers, and Morris the Cat, though very finicky, nevertheless cannot resist Nine Lives cat food.

1900–1925

THE MICHELIN MAN EXEMPLIFIES THE TRAITS THAT HAVE CONTRIBUTED TO THE APPEAL OF ADVERTISING CHARACTERS IN GENERAL. Introduced by the Michelin Brothers in 1898, his anthropomorphic design, a stack of automobile tires with human features, demonstrates the power of iconography. Give a product a face, arms, and legs, and suddenly it becomes more appealing and emotionally accessible—more human. In becoming animate, product images can take on different poses, acquire personality, and be used in a wide variety of advertising media, from point-of-purchase displays

In answering advertisements pleas

Michelin Man • 1910
Michelin tires
Detail of magazine ad

to magazine ads to television commercials. Over the years, hundreds of manufactured and natural objects—from engine pistons to cling peaches—have been graphically "humanized" and registered as trademarks. Like half-human, half-god, Greek mythical beings, consumer culture's anthropomorphic counterparts became half human, half product.

With a successful image in hand, the Michelin Tire Company promoted Bibendum through beautiful lithographic posters—with print runs in the thousands—that graced billboards, motor garages, and shops throughout France and the cities of Europe. Drawn by dozens of the best-known poster artists of the time, the spectacles-wearing, cigar-puffing Bib could be found riding bicycles and racing roadsters. He toasted his competitors with goblets brimming with metal nails and shards of glass to symbolize how well Michelin could imbibe all roadway impediments. He was a lusty fellow who partied, often with a pretty buxom woman at his side, with a particularly French joie de vivre. Bibendum has changed since those early days. He eventually ditched the cigar and spectacles when they no longer represented success and power and gone too are the young ladies. Over the years, his layers of narrow tires have given way to wider, more recognizably modern ones, resulting purposefully in an infantalized and less virile but more friendly and innocent icon.

ntion SCRIBNER'S MAGAZINE

Indeed, many of the earliest ad characters, such as the Michelin Man and the top-hatted Mr. Peanut, wore glasses or carried canes. During post-Victorian times, before celebrity became synonymous with Hollywood movie stars and television-cultivated sports players, celebrity was intimately associated with the aristocracy, or at the very least wealth and power. Many companies, in an effort to set their brand apart from others, used this imagery of good breeding, fine tailoring, and success. Heinz, in an effort to declare its tomato juice as the "classiest" of all tomato juices, introduced Red Magic the Aristocrat Tomato in the 1930s. So too were born John Morrell's tuxedoed Mr. Ham, the discerning tile and floor-covering connoisseur Treadwell Sloane, and the royally crowned King Salad, among countless others. The glamorous cabaret culture of the Art Deco 1920s, as well as America's fascination with butlers and the status they confer, has also served these dapper icons well. In a truly American spin on aristocratic celebrity, the dignified Southern gentleman joined this genre with characters such as Kernel Renk, Judge Arrow, and the real-life Colonel Sanders. As time has gone by, many companies have abandoned these "aristocratic" characters while others have modernized theirs. In the 1960s, Heinz changed the Aristocrat Tomato's name to Tom Tomato, but has rarely used him since. Colonel Sanders, recently contemporized in cartoon style, today performs feats that belie his age and physique. Planter's has transfigured Mr. Peanut's body only slightly since his debut in 1916, and the company still deems him "upscale and classy." But once content to stand casually by his products, this monocled legume, spats and all, now runs and dances in packaging and ads—an effort by Planter's to modernize him. Mr. Peanut is now both a cosmopolitan, club-going "man about town" as well as an approachable, down-to-earth fellow. This transformation is no surprise since the nation's largest snacking group is young buyers.

The success of characters imbued with "personality" (like Bib) did not go unnoticed by advertising agencies, which were first developing as an industry in the early 1900s. Later, the advent of radio and television would allow advertisers to develop more rounded and evolved character traits and story lines for their fictional spokes-characters. And the first self-service supermarkets, like the Piggly Wiggly

Meet Mr Brandyman

He's worth cultivating. Always ready to fit his mood to yours. In the company of ginger ale or soda he offers you the choice of two stimulating and refreshing long drinks.

Make friends with

MARTELL

BRANDY

Mr. Brandyman • 1955
Martell brandy
Magazine ad

chain, which opened in 1916, would give advertisers an added impetus to create memorable Mr. Products to compete for consumers' attention.

Also emulating companies like Michelin, many national advertisers recognized the value of using the best commercial artists of the day to design and illustrate their advertisements in national magazines. As a result, advertising inaugurated a lively tradition of commercial illustration, highlighted by legends such as Paul Rand (Coronet Brandy), Vernon Grant (Kellogg's), A. M. Cassandre (Dubonnet), William Steig (Delco), and Raymond Savignac (BIC). This book pays tribute to their work as well as the work of countless other talented but unheralded graphic artists.

Cartoonish personalities from the illustrators of comic strips and children's books that already possessed name and image recognition, were also appropriated by manufacturers and advertisers. An early example is the Brown Shoe Company's use of Buster Brown and his dog, Tige, who were created by artist Richard Outcault. The visually challenged Mr. Magoo helped promote GE lightbulbs in the 1960s, and the *Peanuts* characters endorse MetLife Insurance today. One of the very first to use ad characters was George Eastman's camera company, later known as Kodak. In 1900, Eastman produced the least expensive camera on the market, the one-dollar Brownie camera. Hoping more children and their parents would be enticed to take up photography due to its low cost, Eastman named it after the little brownie characters created by the Canadian author and illustrator Palmer Cox. By adopting the name and color—the Brownie camera was in fact brown—and using characters already highly popular with children throughout the previous decade, Eastman gained a major marketing advantage over his competitors.

As elfin beings, brownies represented another category of ad characters: magical beings. The ad pantheon is replete with characters based upon German elves, English pixies, and Irish leprechauns—the Spearmint Kid, Ping the Pixie, and the Lucky Charms Leprechaun, to name a few. While pixies, fairies, and leprechauns are carefree spirits, elves are the worker bees of the magical kingdom. This fact, and the now-ingrained American folklore of busy Christmas elves, has made elves a favorite of advertisers.

Psyche the White Rock Girl • 1947
White Rock soda
Detail of promotional booklet

Advertisers used magical characters whenever they wished to suggest that their products could perform effortlessly— in other words, like "magic." Wizards, genies, and magical clowns fill the annals of advertising, pitching products from household cleansers to kitchen appliances. These magical characters were even used to promote many technologically advanced products, such as the automatic garage-door Genie (which is still with us today) and the Facit calculator Wizard. Some advertising characters borrowed directly from classical mythology. These immortal, otherworldly beings suggested a superior product to the consumer— White Rock Soda's Psyche the nymph, Mobil Oil's Pegasus, FTD's Mercury-like wing-footed messenger, and the Ajax White Knight, inspired by King Arthur.

Folklore provides a rich source for ad icons. The Green Giant, for example, was adapted by the Minnesota Valley Canning Company from a fairy tale. The company wanted to publicize the fact that it had developed an uncommonly flavorful and tender "giant"-size pea. The initial giant, introduced in 1925, wore a scowl and a scruffy bearskin and wasn't even green—he was white! Although the company logically made their giant green two years later, it was not until 1935 that the young Chicago ad man Leo Burnett gave him his appealing trustworthy personality and set him in an idyllic valley. In 1968, the Green Giant was joined by his talkative elfin friend, Sprout. A Green Giant magazine ad from 1940, entitled "How the Green Giant Was Born," illustrates how *Grimm's Fairy Tales*, the "Legend of Paul Bunyan," and the tale of "Indian Spirit of Hiawatha-land" all influenced the genesis of the trademark. While some may look at the present-day, arms-akimbo icon and see a buff comic book hero, one can also appreciate that the Green Giant is in some sense a modern-day harvest god, a personification of the correlation between vegetables and good health.

Advertising characters and their story lines share similarities with folk tales and even mythology. Like folk tales, they are a source of entertainment, and like myths, they can typify a culture's valued qualities such as strength and excellence. One must keep in mind however that most advertising, unlike folklore and mythology, is created not to help us understand the universe or even make us better people but to sell products and move merchandise. In fact, advertisements use various clichés and familiar parables whose relationship to a product's benefits, evaluated objectively, is tenuous at best. In a sense, when culture is co-opted to sell and not instruct, advertising characters help to obscure the truth. They become their company's unassailable version of themselves concealing the inner workings of the capitalist system.

1925–1950

BUSINESS BOOMED IN THE MID-1920S—AND SO DID ADVERTISING. Advertising agencies as we know them today were in full gear. Magazines such as the *Saturday Evening Post*, *Collier's*, and *Woman's Home Companion* were chock-full of ads with

Jolly Green Giant • 1947
Green Giant corn
Magazine ad

colorful "Mr. and Mrs. Products." For example, the October 10, 1925, issue of the *Saturday Evening Post* was 260 pages thick. It carried 160 pages of advertising.

After the Great Depression, the American standard of living rose dramatically. Women, as the chief purchasing unit of the household, became the main target of advertising campaigns for consumer products ranging from domestic appliances and cleaning products to ready-made clothing and processed foods. Increasingly, ads appealed to women to become better housewives and superior mothers. Many food companies created fictitious spokeswomen like A&P's Ann Parker, Beatrice Foods' Beatrice Cooke, and of course, Betty Crocker of soon-to-be General Mills.

Betty (named after a popular company vice president named Crocker) was first introduced in 1921 by the forerunner of General Mills, when the Washburn Crosby Company decided it needed a spokeswoman to respond to customers' questions about recipes and baking. *The Betty Crocker Cooking School of the Air* drew millions of radio listeners from 1924 to 1948. By 1936, Betty was given a face, that of the American "everywoman," to go along with her iconic signature. She began appearing in print ads advising families on how to use their limited supplies of money and food to plan wholesome diets during the post-Depression and war years. During this time, *Fortune* magazine named her the second best-known woman in America; only Eleanor Roosevelt was more widely known. The magazine also noted in a 1945 article that at least ten men proposed, by letter, to Betty Crocker! Gradually and subtly, Betty's image has been contemporized over the years to broaden her appeal and to establish rapport not only with homemakers but also with businesspeople—women and men alike.

Betty Crocker's rise to fame was in part due to her widely successful radio program. During the mid-1920s and 1930s, radio emerged as the major advertising medium. It quickly became part of American life, reaching and influencing more people than any other medium. In 1926, the National Broadcasting Company (NBC) was born, and a year later the Columbia Broadcasting System (CBS) came into existence. America began the 1930s with twelve million radio sets and ended the decade with fifty-one million. Radio brought a voice and personality to ad characters.

Elsie • c. 1955
Borden dairy products
Promotional store sign

Borden's Elsie the Cow was another advertising spokes-character who got her big break on radio. She first appeared in 1936 as just another pretty cow in a series of Borden print ads in medical journals. Featured among a variety of cows named Bessie, Clara, and Miss Blossom, Elsie extolled the purity of Borden's condensed milk. When similar ads were run as commercials on local network radio, Elsie's amusing spots became so popular that Borden singled her out as its one and only spokes-cow. In 1939, she made her national debut in consumer magazines, at the

New York World's Fair, and on Borden milk-bottle caps. By 1941, Elsie's cartoon print-ad depictions had given up all pretense of her being just an ordinary, four-legged cow. Since she could already talk, she might as well stand up, too. She became the happy mixture of personified cow and average American housewife, doting on her husband, Elmer (of glue fame), and children, Beulah and Beauregard. Since Borden is a maker of dairy products, the selection of a cow was an obvious one, but there also are more powerful symbolic and subliminal messages built into this half-bovine, half-human image—the milk of human kindness, fertility, and motherhood as well as the nurturing relationship between humans and animals. In fact, the popularity of animal-ad mascots can partly be explained by the psychology of American pet-mania in general. Studies show that the mere presence of animals makes humans (and their companies, in the case of ad characters) seem more trustworthy. From wise owls to kindly pink elephants, the ad world is filled with personified critters. Perhaps ad mascots, whether animal or vegetable, appeal to us because they don't connote the materialism that, in our cynicism, we often associate with their corporate owners.

During World War II, the government turned to the advertising industry for help with, among other things, armed forces recruiting, preventing forest fires, and salvaging scrap metal. Thus characters such as Rosie the Riveter, Smokey the Bear, and Vicky Victory were born. The frugality necessitated by first the Depression and then wartime rationing also gave rise to characters associated with thrift and cost savings. Often wearing tartan kilts and hats, and bearing Scottish-sounding names like Scotty McTape, these thrifty pitchmen and pitchwomen, who would be considered stereotypical today, were plentiful in magazine ads and product labels during World War II.

Vicky Victory • c. 1944
Victory hairpins
Cover of hairpin kit box

Kool Penguin • 1945
Kool cigarettes
Promotional poster

1950–1975

THE GREAT ECONOMIC GROWTH OF THE UNITED STATES FROM 1950 TO 1975 PRODUCED AN ABUNDANCE OF NEW FOOD PRODUCTS AND HOME APPLIANCES—AND EVEN NEWER WAYS TO ADVERTISE THEM. Many GI's returning from the war settled in newly built suburbs with their young families. New housing-starts increased almost 50 percent during this time. Along with the split-level homes and two-car garages came increased energy consumption, automatic dishwashers, air conditioners, and refrigerators filled with frozen vegetables and TV dinners. These developments, as well as the rise of new food technology, generated a host of new ad personalities, such as Teddy Snow Crop for frozen orange-juice concentrate and the Robot Rooter, the "in-sink-erator" garbage disposal unit. Filled with anthropomorphic nails, screws, and lumber, ads in magazines such as *Sunset* and *Better Homes and Gardens* were a testament to the nascent home-improvement industry.

More than the migration to suburbia, however, the 1950s heralded a development that forever changed the world of advertising and American life: television.

The power of TV as an advertising medium quickly superseded radio and print. Television upped the ante: Mr. Product needed to be more than he had ever been before. A successful character needed style, personality, mannerisms, a distinctive one-of-a-kind voice, and even a jingle. (One could say that ad characters were held to the same standards and weeding-out process as were real-life 1940s radio personalities, not all of whom made a successful transition to TV.) One thing, however, was clear: TV made ad characters true celebrities.

Early TV commercials were mainly crude, live testimonials offered by program hosts. Since most ad characters were fictional, initially only those characters that could be personified by performers in costumes—such as the dancing packs of Old Gold Cigarettes—appeared. Live ads were soon replaced by filmed ads. Filmed ads, however, were expensive to produce, and many companies found animation to be a cheaper option. Animation proved very successful for advertising characters because its reality-altering effects gave fictional product spokes-characters their own unique stage on which to entertain and sell their wares. And so early TV animated personalities—the Ajax Pixies, Sharpie the Gillette Blue Blades parrot, the Friskies Dog (a suave canine master of ceremonies who sported a bow tie and boutonniere), and others—were born. Viewers responded with great enthusiasm to the commercials of Mr. Clean, the Hamm's Bear, Captain Raid, and Hey, Mabel! of Carling's Black Label beer campaign.

On the stylistic front, the pen strokes of many commercial illustrators were influenced by a postwar modernism that admired the simple yet elegant structures found in nature. As a result, amorphous-shaped, big-headed, off-beat-looking characters began appearing in magazines ads. They were defined by their simple, squiggly black outlines and sparsely abstract backgrounds—often nothing more than geometric shapes and splashes of color. Animators of commercials were influenced as well. Up until the late 1940s, animation had been locked into a formula established by Walt Disney Studios. Most cartoons were carefully airbrushed with lush colors, staged with hyperrealistic backdrops, and

Old Gold King Size • 1953
Old Gold cigarettes
Detail of magazine ad

executed with smooth animation. But one studio, United Productions of America (UPA), pioneered the introduction of modern designs, developing offbeat commercials that lent themselves visually to the gray-scale limitations of black-and-white television.

Ad characters also reflected America's cultural fascinations. TV westerns (there were thirteen of them in the 1959 season) such as *Gunsmoke* and *Wagon Train* spawned gun-toting, ten-gallon-hat-wearing cowboy wanna-bes such as Buffalo Bee, the Frito Kid, and Marky Maypo. Speedy Alka-Seltzer, blasting off from Cape Canaveral into outer space, and many other previously earthbound characters donning glass-bubble space helmets and silver space suits were simply hitching a ride on the nation's burgeoning space program.

TV comedy teams such as Abbott and Costello and Jackie Gleason and Art Carney of *The Honeymooners* gave rise to fictional comedic partners such as Mo and Par for Mopar auto parts, Col and Gate for Colgate toothpaste, and Bert and Harry Piel for Piel Bros. Brewing Company. The Piels Beer commercials, produced by UPA, were given their voice and comedic improvisation by the real-life comedy team of Bob and Ray, who also lent their improvised humor to other commercial duos like the Peasoup Andersen's "Soup Twins," Hap-Pea and Pea-Wee.

As the 1950s came to a close, ad characters were still going strong, filling magazine ads, store displays, package labels, and mail-away premiums. Some characters made the successful transition to TV stardom while many others from regional and small-business enterprises remained happily content waving from their roadside neon signs and smiling from menu and matchbook marquees.

Many of the ad characters most loved by the baby-boomer generation made their debut during the 1960s. The Pillsbury Doughboy, StarKist's Charlie the Tuna, the Frito Bandito, and Hawaiian Punch's Punchy all appeared during this time.

TV was, if anything, even more influential in the 1960s, leading to the renaissance of Mr. Product. Small-town eccentrics in popular comedies such as *The Andy Griffith Show*, *The Beverly Hillbillies*, and *Green Acres* paved the way for the success of nonanimated personalities such as Josephine the Plumber, who gave a thumbs-up

Tony and "friend" on the Garry Moore Show

Garry Moore says: "Won't they tell even <u>you</u>, Tony?"

Tony: No, the Kellogg's folks won't tell me, or anyone, how they make their special sugar frosting. But I could be persuaded to reveal . . .

Garry: Go on, go on — tell your old pal, Gare . . .

Tony: Well, O.K. Kellogg's secret sugar frosting makes these crisp flakes of corn gr-r-reat for breakfast and . . . here try 'em yourself for a snack.

Garry: Amazing! No wonder so many people enjoy —

Tony: Enjoy Kellogg's Sugar Frosted Flakes? Well, I should say they do. Confidentially, they're the . . . here, try some more.

Garry: Very generous of you, Mr. T. M-m-m-man! These *ARE* the *GREATEST!*

Kellogg's SUGAR FROSTED FLAKES

Tony the Tiger • 1955
Kellogg's Sugar Frosted Flakes cereal
Magazine ad

29

for Comet Cleanser; Mr. Whipple, the nebbish storekeeper who beseeched, "Ladies, please don't squeeze the Charmin"; and Madge the manicurist, who advised her clients to use Palmolive dishwashing liquid. Character actors with inventive personalities proved at times to be as charming (or annoying) as their animated counterparts.

In addition, *The Addams Family* and *The Munsters* influenced General Mills' line of monster-cereal characters, such as the quarreling Count Chocula and Franken Berry, and the James Bond–derived *The Man from U.N.C.L.E.* inspired "The Man from Glad," an espionage agent who saved women from stale sandwiches with the help of Glad's "fold-lock top."

It was, however, the Saturday morning cartoon commercials where ad characters made their biggest impact. In the 1950s, it was still popular to portray breakfast as a traditional family meal. By the 1960s, there was a new head of the breakfast table—kids. More mothers were working than ever before, and fathers were rushing out for the morning commute. But who needed grown-ups when you could eat breakfast with the Trix Rabbit, Cap'n Crunch, Quisp, and Quake? TV commercials were so important in selling cereal that the Quaker Oats Company developed the Cap'n Crunch character before the final formulation of the cereal had even been decided. In addition to the colorful commercials and fantasy-inducing cereal-box images, characters were also promoted via mail-away premiums and "surprise inside" prizes, a formula for success that exists to this day.

Fueling the surge of child-appealing ad characters was the ascendance of the fast-food restaurant in American life. Franchises such as Big Boy, Burger King, Burger Chef, and Jack in the Box brought us their friendly character logos on signage, napkins, and children's meal containers. And, of course, there was Ronald McDonald, who, according to the company, is today recognized by 96 percent of American children.

Interestingly, by the close of the 1960s, the number of magazine advertisements featuring ad characters had declined significantly. Illustration and strong graphics, which had long dominated the appearance of most magazine advertising, were replaced almost totally by photography, which generated a completely different

oot-fray
oops-lay

**(That's Toucan talk for a new cereal
grownups call Froot Loops)**

**Real fruit flavors – orange – lemon – cherry
in a sugar-crystalled oat cereal**

It tastes like fruit, and goes "crunch" to boot! That's
Kellogg's new FROOT-flavored LOOPS—crunchy little circles of cereal,
zinged up with natural orange, lemon, and cherry flavors. Spangled up with
big sugar crystals. Stoked up with important oat nourishment. They're at
your grocer's now—pick up a package for your family this week sure.

Kellogg's **Fr⚬⚬t** FLAVORED **Loops**

Toucan Sam • 1963
Fruit Loops cereal
Magazine ad

31

feel. Companies with ad characters shifted their print advertising focus to news-papers, particularly to colorful Sunday inserts where illustrated and cartoonish char-acters became an integral part of redeemable coupon promotions for breakfast items, processed foods, and household cleansers. Also, many of the general-interest magazine giants such as the *Saturday Evening Post*, *Collier*'s, and *Look* were declin-ing and would fold completely by the end of the 1970s. This signaled the end of the golden age of ad-character magazine illustration, that time when it was the norm rather than the exception for a company to use an ad icon in its promotions.

In the 1970s, corporate trademarks were simplified, becoming more abstract. With the growth of multinational corporations and the proliferation of corporate mergers, company names were shortened, and some ad characters that had once colorfully and boldly graced product labels and stationery were modified to stark, stylized, monotoned semblances of their former selves.

Corporate influences infiltrated ad characters in other ways. Less than one year after *Ms.* magazine debuted in 1971, General Mills, wanting someone who was just as comfortable in the boardroom as the dining room, offered Betty Crocker a red business suit. Unlike their predecessors of the two previous decades, animal charac-ters of the '70s were far less entertaining. Sometimes, for example, they fulfilled the difficult function of representing financial service firms that did not lend themselves to amusing antics. Characters such as the Dreyfus Lion, the Merrill Lynch Bull, and the Hartford Stag were presented as dignified and powerful, and were represented by real animals in commercials. A growing sensitivity to overconsumption, particularly health consciousness, also facilitated the physical slimming of graphic spokes-characters such as the chubby Big Boy, the buxom Sun Maid Raisin Girl, and the cherubic Campbell Kids, and saw a more fit and muscular Tony the Tiger.

Although the decade saw a decline in new characters, some successful kid characters, such as the Freakies cereal clan, were still being developed. Mixing elfin and monster elements with aspects of the waning hippie movement, the un-usual Freakies captured 2 percent of the ready-to eat cereal market. The highly competitive fast-food burger realm in the 1970s brought to TV a humanized magical monarch called the Burger King, who levitated onion rings to compete with McDonald's popular clown, Ronald.

The use of ad characters today is not as pervasive as it was in the 1950s, 1960s, or 1970s. Although still popular, they have not achieved the diversity and originality of the characters of that earlier period. Advertising today is sophisticated and the characters in the ads are now less naïve, as is the public. Since we know we are advertising targets, and advertisers know we know, advertisers—still, of course, with marketing purpose intact—use spoof and tongue-in-cheek humor to get their message across. Joe Isuzu, the sleazy car salesman, hawks his wares and we are amused—and still buy Isuzu cars. The Taco Bell Chihuahua, capitalizing on the theory of advertisers using subliminal messages, brazenly attempts to hypnotize us so we'll eat at Taco Bell.

At the same time, twenty-first-century corporations have begun to appreciate that spokes-characters from the golden age have developed their own cultural heritage, that consumers have a familiarity and comfort level with these characters that are priceless. These days a warm breeze of nostalgia is blowing down Madison Avenue as advertising agencies bring back characters, slogans, and jingles from the 1960s and 1970s. These campaigns are called "retrobranding." Ad agencies realize that although it took a long time to establish these characters, once entrenched in the American psyche, they continue to be a valuable resource for product identification and promotion. Despite the constant pressure in advertising for new, innovative, and trendy icons, marketers are now acknowledging and successfully utilizing the "golden oldies" of earlier times.

1

MEET

Miss Fluffy Rice

ADVERTISERS OFTEN RELY ON THE EMOTIONAL APPEAL OF AD CHARACTERS TO HELP SELL THEIR FOOD PRODUCTS. Give a vegetable or sausage a face and legs and it becomes animate and emotionally accessible—more human. From aristocratic string beans to friendly frankfurters, advertisers have applied the power of anthropomorphic iconography to portray and distinguish their brands.

Foodstuffs such as fish, fowl, and livestock have been given human personalities, too. We find Charlie, a beatnik tuna, to be both funny and poignant in his effort to convince StarKist that he is a worthy candidate for gutting, chopping, and canning. The Piggy Snax hog goes even further—frying up his own skillet of pork rinds.

Characters can also embody a brand's selling point. The Campbell Kids are as wholesome and domestic as the chicken soup they sell. And the buff Jolly Green Giant is the personification of the link between vegetables and good health.

Miss Fluffy Rice • 1960
The Rice Council
Detail of promotional recipe booklet

Marty Mayrose • c. 1967
Mayrose meats
Detail of promotional hand puppet

Little Oscar • 1962
Oscar Mayer wieners
Detail of promotional hand puppet

WISE

potato chips

®

Peppy • c. 1965
Wise potato chips
Promotional store sign

"PEPPY"
®

King Salad • 1938
King Salad avocados
Detail of promotional booklet

Lily Lemon • 1955
Pure Gold Californian lemons
Promotional store display

Ozzie Orange • 1955
Pure Gold Californian oranges
Promotional store display

Kernel Renk • 1970
Renk corn seeds
Detail of promotional booklet

Easy • 1960
Stokely canned vegetables
Detail of magazine ad

meet Mr.
Blue Lake

Mr. Blue Lake • 1954
Blue Lake green beans
Detail of magazine ad

Piggy Snax • 1958
Piggy Snax fried pork rinds
Detail of can

Friskies Cat • 1962
Friskies cat food
Detail of magazine ad

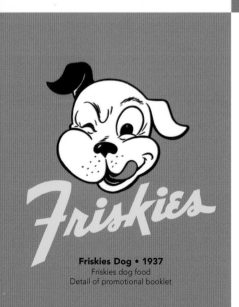

Friskies Dog • 1937
Friskies dog food
Detail of promotional booklet

Bunny • c. 1972
Bunny bread
Detail of promotional hand puppet

Luer Cowboy Pig • c. 1950
Luer meats and sliced bacon
Detail of package

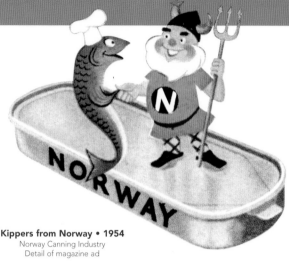

Miss My-T-Fine • 1955
My-T-Fine pie filling
Detail of magazine ad

Bumble Bee • c. 1957
Bumble Bee canned tuna and seafood
Detail of promotional recipe booklet

The Whitman's Messenger • c. 1949
Whitman's chocolates
Cover of box

enger

WY CENTERS
14 OZS. NET WT.

Hot Dan the Mustard Man • 1951
French's mustard
Detail of magazine ad

Rastus • 1954
Cream of Wheat cereal
Detail of magazine ad

45

Kernel Nut of Brazil • 1940
Brazil Nut Association
Promotional paper mask

Sunny Jim • 1939
Force cereal
Promotional paper mask

Tip Top Baker • c. 1951
Tip Top bread
Promotional paper mask

Chief Black Hawk • 1970
Rath Black Hawk meats
Promotional paper mask

Little Oscar • 1962
Oscar Mayer wieners
Promotional paper mask

Fetch • c. 1964
Fetch dog food
Front of box

Each Grain Salutes You • 1948
Uncle Ben's converted rice
Detail of magazine ad

Ken-L-Ration Dog • c. 1957
Ken-L-Ration pet food
Promotional button

Mr. Soybean • 1956
Clara City (MN) Soy Bean Days
Promotional button

Tickle Tim • 1939
Stenzel's Tickle Tim pickles
Lid of jar

Snooty Pea • c. 1949
Kuner's Foods
Promotional store display

Colonel Corn • c. 1949
Kuner's Foods
Promotional store display

Canned Cling Peaches from California

Cling Peaches from California • 1951
Cling Peach Advisory Board
Detail of magazine ad

Nabob Genie • 1972
Nabob tea bags and coffee
Detail of promotional booklet

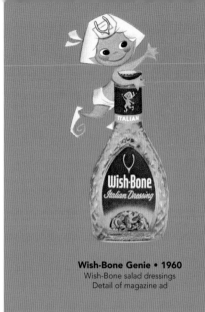

Wish-Bone Genie • 1960
Wish-Bone salad dressings
Detail of magazine ad

Mahatma Genie • 1960
Mahatma rice
Detail of box

The Sarotti Moor • c. 1946
Sarotti chocolates
Promotional store display

Mr. Shiny Fresh • c. 1960
Nut Shelf mixed nuts
Detail of can

Empress Peanut • c. 1960
Empress peanut butter
Detail of can

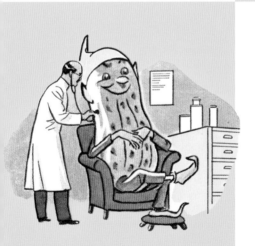

Healthy Peanut • 1946
National Peanut Council
Detail of magazine ad

Hubert the Goober • c. 1945
McColl's peanut butter
Detail of can

Hot Brown Wheatena • 1937
Wheatena cereal
Detail of magazine ad

Slim Chiply • c. 1948
Paramount potato chips
Detail of can

Bertie Bassett • c. 1940
Bassett's Licorice Allsorts candy
Detail of promotional store display

Sue Bee • 1948
Sioux Bee honey
Detail of magazine ad

Chicken of the Sea Mermaid • 1951
Chicken of the Sea tuna
Detail of promotional recipe booklet

Charlie • 1974
StarKist tuna
Promotional playing card

Charlie Chirp • 1940
French's birdseed
Detail of magazine ad

Dinty Moore • 1973
Dinty Moore Hormel beef stew
Detail of promotional coloring book

Frostee • 1960
Lipton Frostee dessert mix
Detail of magazine ad

Golly • c. 1965
Robertson's Golden Shred marmalade
Detail of promotional booklet

Qwip • 1959
Qwip whipped cream
Detail of magazine ad

Citrus Sam • 1949
The National Orange Show
Promotional store display

Star Chef • 1952
Star Italian olive oil
Detail of magazine ad

Choosy the Merry Miller • c. 1958
Pillsbury Best XXXX flour
Detail of magazine ad

Sunshine Baker • 1948
Sunshine biscuits
Detail of magazine ad

La Choy Chef • 1959
La Choy Chinese foods
Detail of promotional booklet

Kraft Salad Man • c. 1978
Kraft salad dressings
Promotional store display

Swifty Frank • 1955
Swift's Premium franks
Detail of magazine ad

Dole Pineapple • 1934
Dole pineapples
Promotional store display

Carey's Pickle • c. 1948
Carey's pickling salt
Detail of promotional recipe booklet

TOM TOMATO
TOURS THE
WORLD OF HEINZ

Tom Tomato • c. 1967
Heinz ketchup and foods
Cover of promotional booklet

2

DRINKS

MEET
Mr. Coffee Nerves

THIRSTY? A BEVY OF BEVERAGE ICONS OFFERED DRINKS TO REFRESH AND CALM US. Soda bottlers designed characters—Bubble Up, Squirt, and Frostie—to fit their effervescent brand names. Importers of liquor often chose playboys, such as the suave Mr. Martell and the rakish Coronet Brandy man, while wholesome girls like Miss Dairylea and Tropic-Ana promoted more domestic, breakfast drinks of milk and orange juice. And if your brand of java kept you awake at night, you could drink non-caffeinated Postum to keep the devilish Mr. Coffee Nerves away!

In the late 1950s, instant drinks with their synthetic sweeteners captured attention and taste buds. The smiling Kool-Aid Pitcher beamed at us from packages sporting rainbows of colors and imitation flavors, while the Fizzies tablet promoted the simplicity and wonder of instant car-bonation. Funny Face's Goofy Grape, Choo Choo Cherry, Jolly Olly Orange, and Rootin'-Tootin' Raspberry joined the fun in the 1960s with bold and colorful pop art graphics.

Mr. Coffee Nerves • 1954
Postum instant hot beverage
Detail of magazine ad

DUBONNET

FORCE
SANTÉ

vin tonique

Dubonnet Man • 1937
Dubonnet aperitif wine
Magazine ad

DUBON
NET

d'après A.M. CASSANDRE 31

u quinquina

DUBONNET

Squirt • 1963
Squirt soda
Promotional decal

ened without sugar!
**TIN'-TOOTIN'
RASPBERRY**

10¢
Makes
2 quarts

Pillsbury's **FUNNY FACE**
ficially sweetened Imitation Drink Mix
Artificial Raspberry Flavor-Dietary
Net Wt. 1/5 (5.7 grams)

Pre-sweetened without sugar!
GOOFY® GRAPE

10¢
Makes
2 quarts

Pillsbury's **FUNNY FACE®**
tificially Sweetened Soft Drink Mix
Artificial Grape Flavor-Dietary
NET WT. 1/5 OZ. (5.7 GRAMS)

Pre-sweetened without sugar!
CHOO CHOO CHERRY

10¢
Makes
2 quarts

Pillsbury's **FUNNY FACE®**
Artificially sweetened Imitation Drink Mix
Artificial Cherry Flavor-Dietary
Net Wt. 1/6 oz. (4.7 grams)

E

0¢
akes
quarts

Pre-sweetened without sugar!
LEFTY® LEMON

10¢
Makes
2 quarts

®

Pillsbury's **FUNNY FACE®**
Artificially Sweetened Soft Drink Mix
Lemon Flavor-Dietary
NET WT. 1/5 OZ. (5.7 GRAMS)

®

rink Mix

Pre-sweetened without sugar!
**FRECKLE FACE
STRAWBERRY**

10¢
Makes
2 quarts

Pillsbury's **FUNNY FACE®**
Artificially sweetened Imitation Drink Mix
Artificial Strawberry Flavor-Dietary
Net Wt. 1/5 oz. (5.7 grams)

Funny Face • 1967
Pillsbury's Funny Face drink mix
Front of packets

Frostie • c. 1961
Frostie root beer soda
Detail of six-pack carrier

Tender Leaf Smiling Cups • 1954
Tender Leaf tea
Detail of magazine ad

Kool-Shake Kids • 1956
Kool-Shake milk shake mix
Detail of magazine ad

Fizzies Tablet • c. 1960
Fizzies instant sparkling drink
Detail of promotional store display

Orange Julius • c. 1968
Orange Julius orange smoothie drink
Promotional store display

Smile • c. 1939
Smile soda
Promotional store display

Fanta Jester • 1963
Fanta orange soda
Detail of magazine ad

Tropic-Ana • c. 1970
Tropicana orange juice
Detail of carton

Miss Freshway • 1936
Freshway beverages
Promotional store display

Keen Kids • 1963
Nestlé's Keen soft drink mix
Detail of magazine ad

CORONET

v.s.q. **BRANDY**

delicious with soda...

with ginger ale...

with your favorite cola

Coronet Brandyman • 1945
Coronet VSQ brandy
Detail of magazine ad

Paul Rand

Ask for
Mr. Sippy

A QUENCHING SLUSH DRINK

SPARKLING
ZIP
IN EVERY
SIP!

Mr. Sippy • c. 1964
Mr. Sippy frozen slush drink
Detail of store sign

Big Shot • 1963
Big Shot chocolate syrup
Detail of can

Judge Arrow • 1957
Arrow liqueurs
Detail of magazine ad

SIX DELICIOUS
CONCENTRATED

Pop Drops • c. 1959
Pop Drops instant sparkling beverage
Detail of packet

Foremost Man • 1971
Foremost liquor stores
Detail of promotional playing card

Hi-Cecil • 1968
Hi-C fruit drink
Detail of can label

Za-Rex Zebra • 1973
Za-Rex citrus punch
Detail of magazine ad

Quik Bunny • c. 1966
Nestlé's Quik strawberry drink mix
Detail of carton

Cocoa Marsh Lion • 1958
Cocoa Marsh chocolate syrup
Detail of soda fountain pump lid

Cinzano Zebra • 1952
Cinzano vermouths and sparkling wines
Promotional poster

Beanie the Genie • 1961
National Federation of Coffee Growers of Colombia
Detail of promotional booklet

Kool-Aid Pitcher • 1966
Kool-Aid soft drink mix
Front of packet

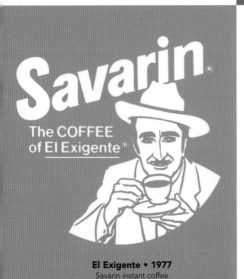

El Exigente • 1977
Savarin instant coffee
Lid of jar

Snap-E-Tom • c. 1972
Snap-E-Tom tomato cocktail
Detail of can

A DOUBLE DIAMOND
works wonders
IND COOPE'S **DOUBLE DIAMOND** BREWED AT BURTON

Double Diamond Man • 1953
Double Diamond beer
Detail of magazine ad

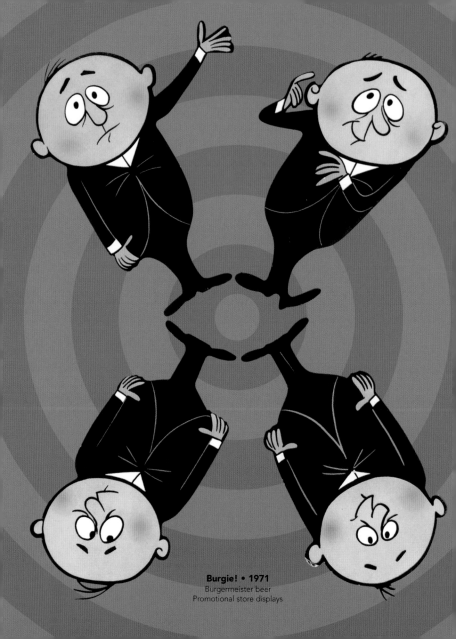

Burgie! • 1971
Burgermeister beer
Promotional store displays

Martini Jockey • c. 1950
Martini vermouth and aperitifs
Detail of restaurant menu

Hamm's Bear • c. 1969
Hamm's beer
Detail of paper cup

Bert and Harry Piel • 1956
Piels beer
Detail of restaurant menu

Marie Brizard • 1961
Marie Brizard anisette liqueur
Detail of magazine ad

Happy Henri • c. 1971
Happy Henri's apple juice
Detail of can label

Cacolac Cow • c. 1970
Cacolac chocolate drink
Detail of promotional store display

© 1961 Quench Co 112-1

Quench • 1961
Quench soda
Promotional decal

King-Size Bubble Up • c. 1958
Bubble Up soda
Promotional decal

Miss Diet Delight • 1955
Diet Delight dietetic foods
Detail of magazine ad

Miss Dairylea • 1958
Dairylea milk and dairy products
Detail of promotional coloring book

Perky • c. 1950
Dr. Pepper soda
Detail of promotional playing card

A&W Bear • 1977
A&W root beer soda
Promotional iron transfer

"Fresh Up" Freddie • 1959
7-Up soda
Detail of promotional booklet

Miss Milkmaid • 1956
Pennsylvania Association of Milk Dealers
Detail of promotional megaphone

ICEE • c. 1970
ICEE frozen carbonated drink
Promotional store display sticker

Mr. Pick Quik • 1959
Nestlé's Quik chocolate drink mix
Detail of promotional game board

Chilly Willee • 1977
Chilly Willee soft ice drink
Detail of promotional button

Teddy Snow Crop • 1955
Snow Crop frozen lemonade
Detail of magazine ad

Mighty Malt • 1987
Budweiser beer
Promotional sticker

The Magic Cow • c. 1971
Magic Cow powdered drink mix
Promotional mixing cup lid

Mochaboy • c. 1958
Mochaboy coffee
Detail of can

Maraca Rum • 1947
Maraca Puerto Rican rum
Detail of magazine ad

Bud Man • 1987
Budweiser beer
Promotional paper mask

3

KIDS' STUFF

KIDS ARE KING TO ADVERTISERS OF CEREALS, SNACKS, CANDY, AND TOYS.

Advertising directed at kids accelerated during early television's unregulated, "anything goes" years of the 1950s and early 1960s. Sponsors often suggested to kids that by eating their cereal or vitamins, they could gain superhuman strength and powers like the Cheerio Kid or Charlie Chocks—or leave their friends choking in a cloud of dust kicked up by their Jets sneakers.

Just like Good and Plenty's Choo-Choo Charlie, a boy or girl could imagine racing a locomotive, or sleeping in an igloo like the kid from Eskimo Pie. TV and movie westerns have made cowboy characters (Buffalo Bee, Twinkie the Kid) a favorite with children. Choruses of "I want my Maypo" and "Silly rabbit!" put products right where advertisers wanted them—on Mom's grocery list.

Mr. Wiggle • 1966
Mr. Wiggle gelatin dessert
Front of box

CHOO-CHOO CHARLIE GAME

Choo-Choo Charlie • 1968
Good and Plenty candy
Detail of promotional game box cover

Campy • c. 1981
Campfire marshmallows
Detail of package

Cracky • 1965
Whitman crayons
Detail of magazine ad

Play-Doh Pete • 1962
Play-Doh modeling compound
Detail of can label

Weather Winky • 1946
Weather Winky children's clothing
Detail of magazine ad

Johnny Jet • 1960
Jets cereal
Detail of magazine ad

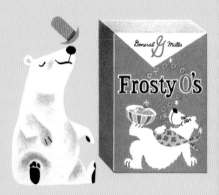

Frosty O's Bear • 1960
Frosty O's cereal
Detail of magazine ad

Corn Kix Kid • 1960
Corn Kix cereal
Detail of magazine ad

Trix Rabbit • 1960
Trix cereal
Detail of magazine ad

Stripey Stripe and Gaylord Giraffe • c. 1961
Stripe toothpaste
Detail of promotional booklet

Stan S. Fluoride • c. 1970
Aim toothpaste
Detail of promotional hand puppet

Mighty White • 1965
Mighty White toothpaste
Detail of box

Bucky Beaver • 1956
Ipana toothpaste
Detail of promotional booklet

Tuffy Tooth • 1969
Colgate toothpaste
Detail of promotional hand puppet

Joe Blo • 1981
Joe Blo bubble gum
Detail of promotional coaster

Dip 'n Sip • c. 1963
Dip 'n Sip chocolate flavored drinking straws
Detail of package

Hubba & Bubba • c. 1985
Hubba Bubba bubble gum
Detail of promotion game box

BEECH-NUT GUM
FRUIT STRIPE
FIVE FLAVORS

BEECH-NUT GUM
CHERRY STRIPE
ARTIFICIAL WILD CHERRY FLAVOR

BEECH-NUT GUM
GRAPE STRIPE
ARTIFICIAL CONCORD GRAPE FLAVOR

The Yipes Stripes Family • 1965
Beech-Nut gum
Detail of promotional coloring book

Captain Cup Cake • c. 1981
Hostess Cup Cakes snack cakes
Promotional store display

Twinkie the Kid • c. 1981
Hostess Twinkies snack cakes
Promotional store display

NEW!

♥ Hostess

ding dongs CAKE

ORANGE
FLAVOR
FROSTING

VITAMIN FORTIFIED

NET WT. 16 OZ. (1 LB.)

King Ding Dong • 1971
Hostess Ding Dongs snack cakes
Cover of box

Snap! Crackle! Pop! • 1933
Kellogg's Rice Krispies
Promotional paper masks

Gobblin' Good Pirate • c. 1976
Carnation ice cream
Promotional paper mask

Good Humor Man • c. 1961
Good Humor ice cream
Promotional paper mask

Scooter Pie Giants • 1967
Burry's Scooter Pie snack pies
Detail of box wrapper

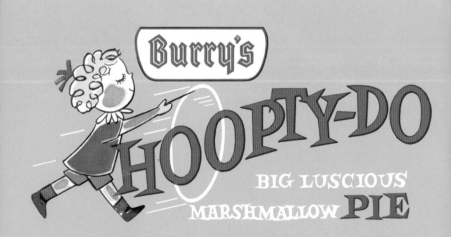

Betsey Burry • 1960
Burry's Hoopty-Do snack pies
Detail of box wrapper

Chesty • 1945
Chesty potato chips
Detail of promotional paper bag

Puddin' Head • 1968
Puddin' Head pudding treat
Detail of package

King Royal • c. 1968
Royal instant pudding
Detail of box

Sparkie • c. 1959
Beverly chunky peanut butter
Detail of jar label

FREE TOY WITH PURCHASE

NET WT. 12 OZ.

25-30 BATHS PER BOX

® matey

WITH LANOLIN AND HEXACHLOROPHENE

COMMENDED BY THE CONSUMER SERVICE BUREAU OF PARENTS' MAGAZINE

PLEASE READ DIRECTIONS FOR USE ON SIDE OF BOX

SOAKS CHILDREN CLEAN AUTOMATICALLY

Matey Mates • c. 1965
Matey bubble bath
Front of box

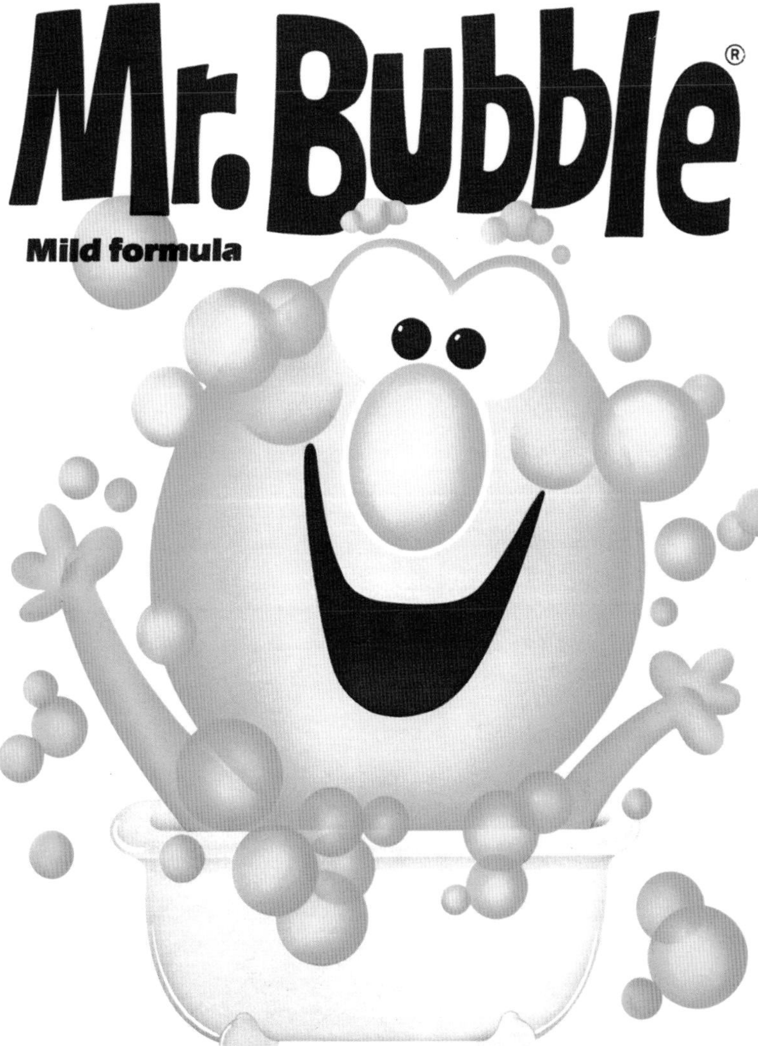

Mr. Bubble • 1966
Mr. Bubble bubble bath
Front of box

Buffalo Bee • c. 1962
Wheat Honeys and Rice Honeys cereal
Detail of magazine ad

Ping the Pixie • c. 1952
Ping the Pixie candy
Detail from box

Mister Softee • 1965
Mister Softee ice cream
Ice cream truck decal

Popsicle Kid • 1940
Popsicle Space-Shots ices
Detail of magazine ad

Cheerios Kid • c. 1966
Cheerios cereal
Detail of comic book ad

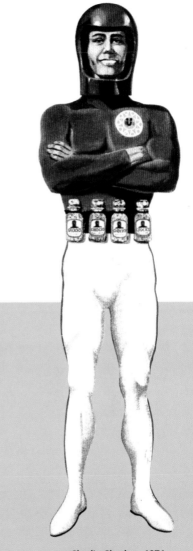

Charlie Chocks • 1971
Chocks multiple vitamins
Detail of package header card

Spearmint Kid • 1965
Wrigley Spearmint gum
Cover of promotional pop-up booklet

Frito Kid • 1954
Fritos corn chips
Promotional store display

Mr. Cool • 1965
Sealtest ice cream
Detail of magazine ad

Weather-Bird • 1958
Weather-Bird children's shoes
Detail of promotional comic book

Jifaroo • c. 1969
Jif peanut spread
Detail of promotional kite

Twinkles • 1960
Twinkles cereal
Detail of promotional sponge

The Most Useful Protein • 1962
Life cereal
Detail of magazine ad

N-R-G Kid • 1936
Curtiss Baby Ruth candies
Detail of box cover

Mr. Yo-Yo • 1960
Duncan yo-yos
Detail of package label

Mr. Dee-lish • 1950
ABC popcorn
Detail of popcorn container

Birds Eye Kids • 1958
Birds Eye frozen foods
Promotional store display

Eskimo Pie Kid • c. 1957
Eskimo Pie toasted almond bars
Detail of promotional store display

Clark Bar Kid • c. 1960
Clark candy bars
Cover of box

Marky Maypo • 1961
Maypo oat cereal
Promotional button

Freakies • 1987
Freakies cereal
Promotional sticker

Bazooka Joe • c. 1957
Bazooka bubble gum
Promotional button

Frito Bandito • 1970
Fritos corn chips
Promotional button

Tony the Tiger • c. 1966
Kellogg's Sugar Frosted Flakes cereal
Promotional button

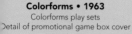

Colorforms • 1963
Colorforms play sets
Detail of promotional game box cover

Hasbro Kid • 1959
Hasbro toys
Detail of toy box

Transy • 1962
Transogram toys and games
Detail of toy catalog

Whitman Kid • 1979
Whitman books
Detail of book cover

Matty Mattel • 1965
Mattel toys
Detail of magazine ad

Franken Berry • 1990 ➤
Count Chocula • 1990
Boo Berry • 1998
Yummy Mummy • 1990
General Mills monster cereals
Front of cereal boxes

Pals'

Club
Member

Pals • 1969
Pals vitamins
Detail of promotional mug

Quake and Quisp • 1965
Quake and Quisp cereals
Cover of promotional comic book

Milton the Toaster • 1973
Pop Tarts toaster pastries
Detail of promotional puzzle

Sugar Crisp Bear • 1961
Post Sugar Crisp cereal
Front of cereal box

Mr. Neolite • 1957
Neolite shoe soles
Detail of magazine ad

Swifty Flyer • c. 1962
P. F. Flyer sneakers
Detail of promotional store display

Jets Astro Kid • 1959
Red Ball Jets sneakers
Promotional store display

4

DINING

MEET
Mister DONUT

Mister DONUT

Mister DONUT *

HOT DOGS, BURGERS, FRIED CHICKEN—since everyone must eat, what could be more inviting to a traveling family than a happy chef or beckoning ice-cream cones with smiling faces? Roadside ad characters are among the most memorable icons.

The earliest classics were the brainchildren of diners and drive-ins such as Bob's Big Boy, Chicken in the Rough, and Howard Johnson's. These were soon followed by the 1950s' California-style coffee shops like The Bun Boy, Biffs, and Loop's. Quick-stop donut shops were happy to serve up their icons with donut faces or bodies. Dunkin' Donuts even had a trademark that had crullers for arms and legs.

Then there were the fast-food franchises like Burger King and Jack in the Box whose advertising namesakes transfigured over the years from elfin to human form. Some mascots (like Pioneer Pete and Burger Chef) disappeared when their franchises folded, but others (Wendy, Colonel Sanders) are still going strong.

Mister Donut • 1955
Mister Donut coffee and donuts shops
Detail of matchbook

Dunkie • 1956
Dunkin' Donuts shops
Promotional store display

Spudnuts • 1951
Spudnuts donut shops
Detail of magazine ad

Winchell's Donut • c. 1963
Winchell's Donut House donut shops
Detail of paper cup

Dixie Cream Donut • c. 1946
Dixie Cream donut shops
Detail of magazine ad

Danny Donut • 1937
Mayflower Hot Donuts shops
Promotional store display

STEREO

DOG n SUDS *Presents . . .*

By the time I get to Phoenix

Rover • c. 1969
Dog n Suds drive-in restaurants
Detail of promotional album jacket

Doggie Diner • c. 1970
Doggie Diner restaurants
Detail of hot dog wrapper

Superdawg • 1948
Superdawg drive-in restaurant
Detail of hot dog serving box

Pizza Pete • 1969
Pizza Hut restaurants
Cover of matchbook

Long John Silver • c. 1970
Long John Silver's seafood restaurants
Detail of promotional hand puppet

Der Wienerschnitzel • c. 1970
Der Wienerschnitzel restaurants
Detail of promotional hand puppet

Captain D • 1974
Captain D's restaurants
Cover of restaurant menu

Big Boy • 1950
Bob's Big Boy restaurants
Cover of restaurant menu

Ronald McDonald • c. 1966
McDonald's restaurants
Promotional hand puppet

Burger King • 1972
Burger King restaurants
Promotional hand puppet

Skychef • c. 1965
Skychef airport restaurants
Cover of matchbook

Shakey's Pizza Chef • 1966
Shakey's pizza parlors
Cover of matchbook

White Tower Chef • 1946
White Tower restaurants
Cover of matchbook

Frey's Favorite • c. 1948
Frey's wieners
Cover of matchbook

Horn & Hardart Chef • c. 1948
Horn & Hardart automats
Cover of matchbook

The Champ • c. 1959
Jack's drive-in restaurants
Detail of matchbook

Globe • c. 1948
Globe coffee shops
Cover of matchbook

Ole • c. 1953
Ole's Waffle Shop restaurants
Cover of matchbook

Speedee • 1958
McDonald's restaurants
Detail of paper cup

The Burger King • 1976
Burger King restaurants
Detail of promotional hand puppet

Burger King • 1966
Burger King restaurants
Detail of magazine ad

Archie McDonald • 1964
McDonald's restaurants
Detail of promotional puzzle game

THE
BURGER FAMILY

The Burger Family • 1960
A&W drive-in restaurants
Detail of store sign

OSCAR

Oscar • c. 1961
Oscar's drive-in restaurants
Promotional paper mask kids' menu

The Little Chef • c. 1956
The Park Pantry restaurant
Promotional paper mask kids' menu

Sambo • c. 1972
Sambo's restaurants
Promotional paper mask

Tiger • c. 1972
Sambo's restaurants
Promotional paper mask

Pig'n Whistle • c. 1947
Pig'n Whistle restaurant
Promotional paper mask

Hi Boy • c. 1970
Hi Boy restaurants
Detail of restaurant menu

Big Boy • c. 1961
Frisch's Big Boy restaurants
Detail of matchbook display tray

Bun Boy • c. 1957
The Bun Boy restaurant
Cover of matchbook

Happy Boy • c. 1960
Happy Boy restaurant
Detail of matchbook

Tasty Boy • c. 1950
Hasty Tasty drive-in restaurants
Detail of restaurant menu

Burger Chef • c. 1968
Burger Chef restaurants
Detail of promotional hand puppet

Colonel Sanders • 1952
Kentucky Fried Chicken restaurants
Detail of bucket lid

Jack in the Box • 1976
Jack in the Box restaurants
Detail of promotional album jacket

Happy Star • 1974
Carl's Jr. restaurants
Detail of promotional album jacket

Burger Chef • 1977
Burger Chef restaurants
Detail of burger serving box

GR-R-REAT FOOD!

Sambo's
RESTAURANTS

Sambo • c. 1972
Sambo's restaurants
Promotional postcard

Biff's Chef • 1965
Biff's coffee shops
Detail of restaurant menu

Pioneer Pete • 1978
Pioneer chicken restaurants
Detail of restaurant table sign

Dunkie Donut-Head • 1967
Dunkin' Donuts shops
Cover of promotional toy box

Sizzler • 1966
Sizzler restaurants
Detail of restaurant bib

Wendy • c. 1980
Wendy's restaurants
Promotional hand puppet

Dixie Lee • c. 1960
Dixie Lee fried chicken restaurants
Detail of promotional coin bank

Miss Dairy Queen • 1963
Dairy Queen stores
Detail of promotional coloring book

Little Miss Loops • c. 1972
Loop's restaurants
Detail of matchbook

Mr. Steak • 1970
Mr. Steak restaurants
Promotional hand puppet

Taco Bell Kid • 1968
Taco Bell restaurants
Promotional paper mask

The Jolly Roger • c. 1966
The Jolly Roger restaurants
Promotional paper mask kids' menu

Coco's Spaceman • c. 1958
Coco's restaurants
Promotional paper mask kids' menu

DON'T COOK TONIGHT call CHICKEN DELIGHT

Chicken Delight • c. 1970
Chicken Delight take-out restaurants
Detail of restaurant menu

Acey Bird • 1966
Arctic Circle drive-in restaurants
Detail of promotional coloring book

Pixie • 1969
The Pixie Kitchen restaurant
Detail of promotional postcard

Tee and Eff • 1957
Tastee-Freez restaurants
Detail of promotional gift box

Hap-Pea and Pea-Wee • 1954
Pea Soup Andersen's restaurants and soups
Detail of promotional recipe booklet

Waddle's Duckling • c. 1959
Waddle's restaurant
Detail of burger wrapper

Little Foster • 1965
Foster Freeze drive-in restaurants
Detail of company newsletter

Insta Burger King • 1955
Insta Burger King drive-in restaurants
Detail of magazine ad

Chef Frialator • 1955
Pitco Frialator fryers
Detail of magazine ad

Pappy Parker • 1973
Pappy Parker's Chicken Barn restaurants
Detail of fried chicken serving box

5

TECHNOLOGY

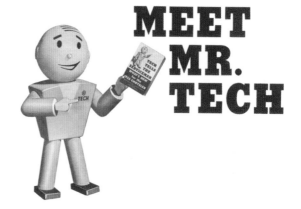

TECHNOLOGY HAS OFFERED A VERY FERTILE FIELD FOR ADVERTISING ICONS.

What better way to demystify advancements in electricity, communications, and computer science than to "personify" thunderbolts, transistors, and computer chips. Utilities, too, have made great use of these humanized creatures with such icons as Handy Heat, Willie Wiredhand, and Miss Penny Flame, giving power companies likable diplomats to offer safety tips and remind citizens to pay their heating bills.

Graphic designers, called upon to fashion their company's newest vision of tomorrow, often chose the robot as an ad character. Even prior to Westinghouse Corporation's introduction of Elektro and his robot dog Sparko at the 1939 World's Fair, the robot symbolized advanced technology, automation, and a better, toil-free future through science.

Not to be forgotten are the genies and wizards, who present industry's "automatic" products as wondrous and magical. These characters were designed to convince consumers that ordinary repetitive tasks such as opening a garage door or turning on the lights would be much easier and more fun using their devices.

Mr. Tech • 1954
Chrysler Master Technician Conference
Detail of service manual

Power Mite • c. 1965
General Electric Power Mite flashbulbs
Detail of package

SYLVANIA'S MR. LIGHT ™

Mr. Light • 1985
Sylvania lightbulbs
Detail of promotional night-light

Randy the Transistor Radio • 1963
Sony transistor radios
Detail of promotional booklet

© C.E. CO.

Little Bill • 1955
Commonwealth Edison utility company
Detail of lightbulb package

Ronson Robot • c. 1954
Ronson lighters
Detail of lighter fix-it kit lid

BTU Dee • c. 1947
AFCO furnaces and heaters
Detail of promotional clock

電球は・・・
ナショナル

National Lightbulb Man • c. 1965
Matsushita Electric National lightbulbs
Detail of store sign

KD • c. 1955
Ken Sewell Sales supplies
Detail of promotional ashtray

Rocket Boy • 1969
Rocket batteries
Promotional decal

Mr. Weatherball • c. 1967
Northwestern National banking services
Detail of coin saver booklet

Youngstown Kitchens Waste Disposer • 1953
Youngstown Kitchens equipment and appliances
Detail of magazine ad

Tiny Gas Flame • 1948
Serval gas refrigerators
Detail of magazine ad

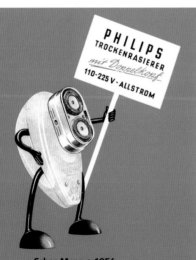

Scher Mann • 1956
Philips electric shavers
Detail of box

Miss Flame • 1947
American Gas Association
Detail of promotional comic book

Reliance Robot • c. 1952
Reliance anti-freeze
Detail of can

G-E Bulb • 1945
General Electric lightbulbs
Promotional store display

Mr. Civil Defense • c. 1955
Civil Defense Week promotion
Promotional poster

Kraft TV Cameraman • 1954
Kraft Television Theatre program
Detail of promotional coloring book

Chevy Robot • c. 1955
Chevrolet service and parts
Detail of promotional ashtray

Elektro and Sparko • 1940
New York World's Fair Westinghouse exhibit
Promotional button

Swifty Service • 1959
Black & Decker tools
Detail of magazine ad

Mr. Benzie • 1965
Dermik benzoyl peroxide acne lotion
Detail of trademark registration document

Mr. Magnaflux • c. 1966
Magnaflux inspection and testing equipment
Detail of promotional ashtray

Red Ball • 1962
Ingersoll-Rand tools
Detail of magazine ad

Mr. Dumont • 1957
Dumont engine oscilloscopes
Detail of magazine ad

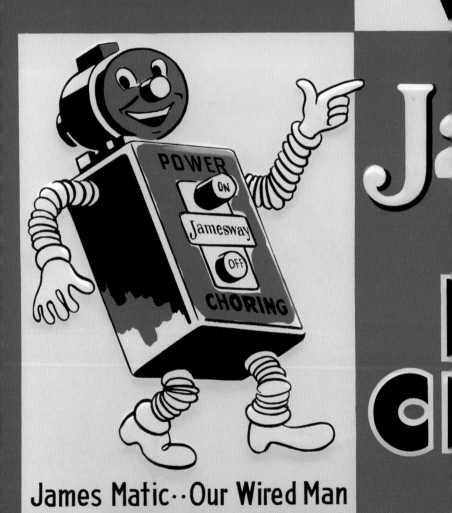

James Matic—Our Wired Man • 1956
Jamesway livestock feeding equipment
Promotional store sign

VE·USE

mesway ®

OWER

RING ®

UIPMENT

Penny Flame • 1963
Northern Illinois Gas utility company
Apartment building sign

Willie Wiredhand • 1951
National Rural Electric Cooperative Association
Detail of lightbulb package

Louie the Lightening Bug • 1984
Alabama Power utility company
Detail of promotional coloring book

Reddy Kilowatt • c. 1980
Reddy Kilowatt Corporation
Promotional iron transfer

Robot Rotor • 1954
In-Sink-Erator food-waste disposer
Detail of magazine ad

Genie • 1966
Genie garage door openers
Detail of promotional clock

Mr. Grasshopper • 1943
Aeronca Grasshopper aircraft
Detail of magazine ad

Oxy • 1960
Marquette oxy-acetylene equipment
Detail of magazine ad

'Get me out of this dump'

says
JACK SCRAP

Jack Scrap • 1952
British Iron and Steel Federation scrap drive
Detail of magazine ad

THE IRON FIREMAN

Iron Fireman • 1953
Iron Fireman furnaces and gas burners
Detail of magazine ad

Smart Repair Detective

Smart Repair Detective • 1960
General Electric electronic tubes
Detail of promotional store display

OHMITE
presents...
two dependable performers✱

Little Devil • 1950
Ohmite Little Devil resistors
Detail of magazine ad

Miss Bell Telephone • 1951
Bell Telephone System promotion
Detail of magazine ad

Facit Wizard • 1961
Facit adding machines
Detail of box

Mr. Bell Telephone • 1941
Bell Telephone System promotion
Detail of magazine ad

Mr. Controls • 1953
Robertshaw automatic oven controls
Detail of magazine ad

I am *Mido**

I am shock resistant and anti-magnetic. Sportsmen, engineers, scientists find me utterly trustworthy.

I am 100% waterproof—unafraid of water, hot or cold, fresh or salt.

Mido • 1950
Mido automatic watches
Detail of magazine ad

174

Mr. B • 1951
Brumberger photographic supplies
Detail of magazine ad

Al Luminum • c. 1960
Kaiser aluminum
Promotional playing card

Stocky Steel • c. 1960
United States Steel metal supplies
Promotional playing card

Mr. P&D • 1959
P&D ignition systems
Detail of magazine ad

I am the Nauga.
I am attached to this because it is covered with my hide—Naugahyde vinyl fabric. Never buy any vinyl fabric unless my picture is hanging on it.

Nauga • 1967
Uniroyal Naugahyde vinyl coated fabric
Promotional tag

Mr. TV Tube • 1960
General Electric electronic tubes
Promotional store display

AMF Genie • c. 1965
AMF Paragon automatic timers
Detail of box

Gas Genie • c. 1957
Greater Winnipeg Gas utility company
Detail of store sign

K-M Electrical Servant • 1951
Knapp-Monarch home appliances
Detail of promotional recipe booklet

Take Me to Your "Litter" • 1959
United trash cans
Promotional button

Midget Pilot • c. 1960
Perfection home heaters
Detail of promotional booklet

NAT • c. 1955
National screws and bolts
Detail of box

Phillips Screw Man • 1942
Phillips recessed head screws
Detail of magazine ad

Mr. Western Electric • 1947
Western Electric telephone system
Detail of magazine ad

Provide more than 2,000,000 telephone lines in 4500 central offices.

Mr. Master Method • c. 1963
Master catalog rack systems
Promotional decal

Danny Thunderbolt • 1955
Plumbing specialty tools
Detail of plastic container

Snappy Service • 1946
Copper and Brass Sales metal supplies
Detail of company envelope

Mr. Rectifier • 1944
General Electric electronic tubes
Detail of magazine ad

Reddie Wilcolator • 1952
Wilcolator gas ovens and ranges
Detail of promotional recipe booklet

Handy Heat • c. 1963
Brooklyn Union Gas utility company
Detail of promotional booklet

Pliofilm • 1947
Goodyear Pliofilm plastic wrap
Detail of magazine ad

6

AUTOMOTIVE

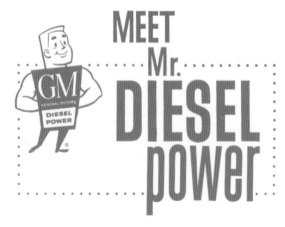

THE AUTOMOBILE, THAT MAINSTAY OF PERSONAL MOBILITY, INSPIRED AN INCREDIBLE ARRAY OF ADVERTISING CHARACTERS. From shock absorbers to piston rings, ignition wires to spark plugs, car parts begged to be personified by their manufacturers.

Oil drops were a particular favorite of makers of motor oil, giving us the internationally famous Esso Oil Drops and the less renowned Pete Penn. More inventive was the 1950s trench-coated detective Bardahl, who rushed to the aid of imperiled motorists—usually beautiful blondes. Offering his motor oil, he foiled the menacing gangsters—the likes of Blackie Carbon, Gummy Rings, and Sticky Valves—living in their car engines.

Gasoline companies capitalized on consumers' undemocratic desire to be waited on with the image of crisp and friendly station crews like the Union 76 Minutemen and the singing Texaco Servicemen. For those who wanted someone to worry about them, Flying A's basset hound, Axelrod, did the honors. And Esso's "Put a tiger in your tank" simultaneously solved the problem of sluggish cars while satisfying the consumers' desire for speed and power.

Mr. Diesel Power • 1960
General Motors engines
Detail of magazine ad

Blacky Carbon

Clatterbad Clara

Gummy Rings

Bardahl • 1955
Bardahl motor oil
Promotional stickers

Sticky Valves

Barney • 1958
Behr-Manning auto tape
Detail of magazine ad

Wynn's Oil Drop • 1953
Wynn's motor oil
Detail of promotional booklet

Bear • 1952
Bear auto alignment service
Detail of promotional ink blotter

Axelrod • 1965
Flying A gasoline
Detail of promotional playing card

AC Oil Drop • c. 1963
AC oil filters
Detail of magazine ad

Poly • c. 1965
Iskenderian Poly Dyne camshafts
Promotional racing decal

Dino • 1966
Sinclair Dino Supreme gasoline
Detail of road map

Offenhauser Turtle • 1962
Offenhauser racing engines
Promotional racing decal

Mr. Horsepower • 1959
Clay Smith camshafts
Promotional racing decal

Mr. Wheelie • 1962
Racing Wheels newspaper
Promotional racing sticker

Mr. Torque • c. 1965
Sturtevant torque wrenches
Promotional racing decal

◄ **Minute Man Servicemen • 1954**
Union 76 gasoline
Detail of road map

Esso Oil Drop • c. 1962
Esso gasoline
Gasoline station rest room sign

Extra Smileage • 1959
B. F. Goodrich Silvertown tires
Detail of magazine ad

Delco Kid • 1959
Delco auto batteries
Detail of magazine ad

Mr. Goodwrench • 1978
General Motors service and parts
Detail of promotional coloring book

Mr. Viz Spark • 1919
Visible spark plugs
Detail of magazine ad

Casey "KC" Piston • 1962
Korody-Colyer pistons
Detail of matchbook

The Grote Sailor • 1957
Grote auto taillights and stoplights
Detail of magazine ad

Empi • 1966
Engineered Motor Products Volkswagen accessories
Promotional racing sticker

Esso Tiger • 1967
Esso gasoline
Promotional decal

Autol Serviceman • c. 1940
Autol Desolite gasoline additives
Gasoline station sign

VW Girl • c. 1969
Volkswagen automobiles
Promotional sticker

OK Serviceman • c. 1960
OK Auto Float tires
Front of promotional coin bank

Wiry Joe® says:

"Start Hitch-Hiking!"

Iskenderian Supercam • c. 1960
Iskenderian racing camshafts
Promotional racing sticker

Sparky • 1958
AC spark plugs
Detail of magazine ad

Hastings Man • 1958
Hastings piston rings
Detail of magazine ad

Jimmy Diesel • 1960
General Motors engines
Detail of promotional booklet

Phil • 1966
Phillips 66 gasoline
Gasoline station sign

Tommy the Turtle • 1955
Turtle Wax auto polish
Detail of can

Pepe Chevron • 1961
Chevron (Mexico) gasoline
Detail of promotional booklet

Ollie • c. 1970
Oliver tractors
Detail of promotional coloring book

Mo and Par • 1957
Mopar automotive parts
Detail of magazine ad

General Ordinance • 1959
Union Carbide auto cooling systems
Detail of magazine ad

Mr. Grey Rock • 1962
Grey-Rock brake linings
Detail of magazine ad

Stringfellow Power • 1959
Stringfellow power wreckers
Detail of magazine ad

Mr. C. P. • 1959
Chicago Pneumatic auto wrenches
Detail of magazine ad

Car-Buoy • 1959
Moog Car-Buoy shock springs
Detail of magazine ad

Sherlock McKanick • 1957
Blue Streak ignition parts
Detail of magazine ad

Puritan • 1962
Puritan brake fluid
Detail of magazine ad

Oscar • 1957
Ausco car jacks
Detail of magazine ad

Elreco Serviceman • 1956
Elreco (El Dorado Refinery Co.) gasoline
Detail of road map

Hancock Rooster • 1948
Hancock gasoline
Detail of road map

Film-Fiter Kid • 1943
Film-Fiter windshield wipes
Detail of magazine ad

Champ • c. 1950
Champion spark plugs
Detail of matchbook

Trusty • 1958
Trostel oil seal rings
Detail of magazine ad

Mr. Allstate • c. 1962
Sears Allstate truck tires
Detail of promotional ashtray

PEP • 1957
Holley carburetors
Detail of magazine ad

Mr. H and Mr. M • 1962
Hinckley Myers auto equipment
Detail of magazine ad

K-D • 1960
K-D truck safety mirrors and lights
Detail of magazine ad

Bibendum • c. 1979
Michelin tires
Promotional store sign

Eager Beaver • 1963
Cities Service gasoline
Promotional paper mask

Popeye • 1939
Chevrolet automobiles
Promotional paper mask

Duster • 1970
Plymouth Duster automobiles
Detail of promotional poster

Octopus • 1966
Octopus car washes
Detail of promotional playing card

Esso Oildrop • 1960
Esso gasoline
Detail of road map

Mighty Mallory • c. 1970
Mallory ignition and fuel system products
Promotional racing sticker

Oklahoma Ethyl • 1955
Oklahoma gasoline
Detail of baseball scorecard

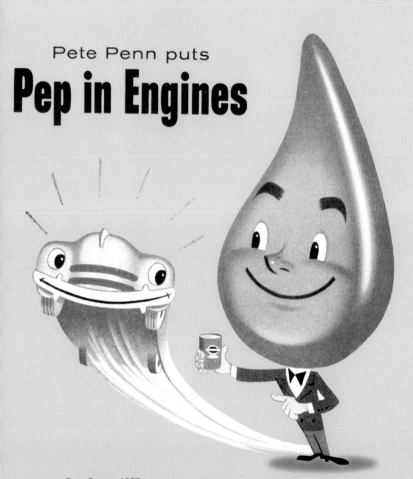

Pete Penn puts
Pep in Engines

Pete Penn • 1957
Pennsylvania motor oil
Detail of magazine ad

The Pep Boys • 1955 ➤
Pep Boys automotive stores and service centers
Cover of sales catalog

Freddy Fast • 1976
Douglas gasoline
Promotional decal

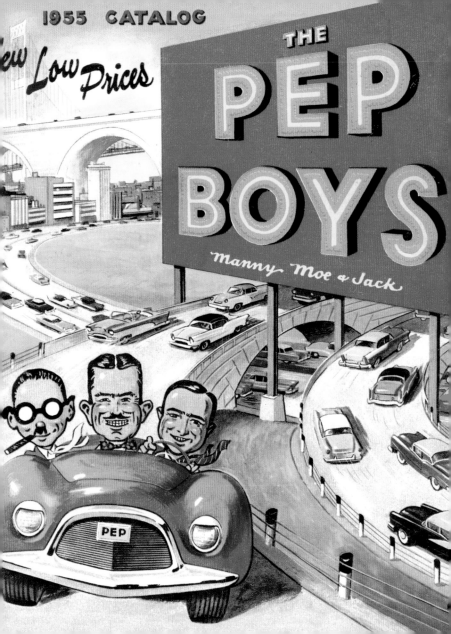

7

HOME

TECHNOLOGY TRANSFORMED THE HOME IN THE TWENTIETH CENTURY, AND A HOST OF AD CHARACTERS BROUGHT THOSE ADVANCES TO NEW HOMEOWNERS. Detergents and cleansers promised to make your sheets "whiter than white" and fabrics "sparkle like new." Mr. Clean, the Dutch Girl, and the Ajax White Knight, who was "stronger than dirt," helped beleaguered housewives with their dirty laundry, dishes, and cleaning chores.

There were also the "miracle" appliances of the 1950s. Miss Mirro-Matic helped you cook faster, and Magic Chef helped you bake better. Lennie Lennox kept you warm at night, and Frigidaire's Thrifty Twin Bears not only kept your room cool but they did it cheaply, too.

The suburban home-building boom in postwar America created its own boom in anthropomorphic ad characters made of building materials, including everything from nails to fiberboards. Along with them came the funny little handymen who cheerfully painted homes, killed bugs, rooted drains, and made your water sparkly clean.

Mr. Happy Homer • 1960
Staggs-Bilt home builders
Detail of company stationery

IL EST ORANGE

ESSAYEZ UN BIC ORANGE. Il vous étonnera. Sa nouvelle bille poli-glace, en carbure de tungstène, glisse toute seule sur le papier. Inusable, elle glisse, glisse jusqu'au dernier mot, sans à-coups ni bavures. 40 % d'écriture en plus. Pour 1 N. F., découvrez la nouvelle écriture BIC !

BIC Boy • 1960
BIC pens
Magazine ad

Mister Ice • c. 1951
Mister Ice canned refrigerant
Front of can

Mr. Treadwell Sloane • 1952
Sloane floor and wall tile
Detail of magazine ad

Mister Master • c. 1955
Master padlocks
Detail of magazine ad

Staple Sam • c. 1942
Staple-Master stapling machines
Detail of promotional ink blotter

Big Red • 1967
Big Red rooter and sewer service
Detail of magazine ad

Renuzit Doozit • 1982
Renuzit air freshener
Detail of package label

General Paint • c. 1948
General paints
Detail of paint-sample booklet

Captain Raid • 1977
Raid House and Garden insecticide
Magazine ad

Captain Raid • 1977
Raid House and Garden insecticide
Magazine ad

Meet His
Royal Nibs___

His Royal Nibs • 1955
Nibroc paper towels
Detail of magazine ad

"Otto" the Orkin Man • 1966
Orkin insect and pest control
Cover of promotional coloring book

Mr. Zip • 1968
U.S. Postal Service zip code promotion
Detail of promotional comic book

Thrifty Twin Bears • 1954
Frigidaire air conditioners
Detail of magazine ad

Lennie Lennox • 1952
Lennox furnaces
Detail of magazine ad

Benny Mautz • c. 1965
Mautz paints
Detail of store display

Molly • 1952
Molly screw anchors
Cover of matchbook

B-E Beaver • c. 1965
Builders Emporium hardware stores
Detail of promotional booklet

Bandi • c. 1959
Bandini fertilizer
Cover of matchbook

The Yard Bird • c. 1960
The Yard Birds Shopping Center
Cover of matchbook

Ajax White Knight • 1968
Ajax detergent
Front of box

Clorox Man • 1957
Clorox bleach
Detail of magazine ad

Mister Bubble Head • c. 1965
Mister Bubble Head lawn sprinkler heads
Detail of promotional store display

Mr. T • 1957
Dixon Ticonderoga pencils
Detail of magazine ad

Hotpoint Pixie • 1954
Hotpoint appliances
Detail of promotional tile

Culligan Man • 1965
Culligan water conditioning services
Cover of promotional coloring book

Toppie the Elephant • 1960
Top Value savings stamps
Promotional store display

Coldspot Penguins • c. 1949
Sears Coldspot refrigerators
Detail of promotional recipe booklet

Baggies Alligator • 1973
Baggies plastic sandwich bags
Detail of carton

Goldie the Gold Seal • 1952
Gold Seal glass wax
Detail of magazine ad

I Just Don't See GE Bug-Lites!

Bug-Lite • 1958
General Electric Bug-Lite lightbulbs
Detail of package

The Rose Man • c. 1963
Rose Exterminator insect and pest control
Detail of promotional store display

US BUGS
SURE HATE
ORTHO!

Ortho Bug • c. 1959
Ortho insecticide
Promotional store display

JOIN THE HEALTH SQUAD

Flit • 1929
Flit insecticide spray
Promotional store display

Mr. Clean-Up • 1946
St. Louis Chamber of Commerce antilitter campaign
Detail of bus pass

Mr. Marks-a-Lot • 1959
Carter's ink and markers
Detail of magazine ad

Mister Magoo • 1960
General Electric lightbulbs
Detail of promotional playing card

IT'S EASY TO SEE THE BEST BULBS ARE G·E

© UPA PICTURES, INC.

234

King Soopers • c. 1953
King Soopers supermarkets
Cover of promotional sewing kit

Stop-n-Shop • c. 1953
Stop-n-Shop supermarkets
Detail of promotional sewing kit

Piggly Wiggly • c. 1950
Piggly Wiggly supermarkets
Cover of promotional sewing kit

Dutch Girl • 1956
Dutch cleanser
Front of can

Arvin Annie • 1951
Arvin toasters and skillets
Detail of magazine ad

Rubbermaid • 1950
Rubbermaid housewares
Detail of magazine ad

Miss Mirro-Matic • 1954
Mirro-Matic pressure cookers
Detail of magazine ad

Super Trim • c. 1967
Super Trim detergent
Detail of promotional card

Texcel Tex • 1949
Texcel tape
Detail of magazine ad

Scotty McTape • 1945
Scotch cellophane tape
Detail of magazine ad

Ivory Snowman • 1951
Ivory Snow soap
Detail of magazine ad

Tommy Mohawk • 1959
Mohawk carpets
Detail of magazine ad

Mister Thinzit • c. 1955
Mister Thinzit paint thinner
Front of can

Fir-Tex • 1955
Fir-Tex acoustical tile
Detail of magazine ad

Wally Wal-Lok • 1959
Wal-Lok mortar joint reinforcing
Detail of magazine ad

Mr. Strut • 1958
Unistrut metal brackets
Detail of promotional sign

Handyman • 1957
The Handyman of California hardware stores
Detail of magazine ad

Western Lumber • c. 1958
Western Lumber stores
Detail of matchbook

8

PERSONAL & LEISURE

"LOOK SHARP! FEEL SHARP! BE SHARP!" advised Sharpie the parrot for Gillette razor blades. Brylcreem claimed "a little dab'll do ya," while Speedy Alka-Seltzer sang, "Plop, plop, fizz, fizz / Oh, what a relief it is!" Johnny Mint made your breath fresher, Little Miss Coppertone your tan darker, and Mighty White your teeth brighter.

Advertising for products to make Americans look good and feel better blossomed in the 1950s and continues to thrive today. Personal-product icons also flourished, reaching beyond toiletries to dry goods and travel. Notable characters like the Levi Cowboy, Hush Puppies, McGregor's Mr. Happy Foot, and Blackie for Cat's Paw soles promoted clothing and footwear.

More disposable income also meant more traveling. You could explore Wisconsin with Bucky Badger. Tour with Tommy Trailways. Rest well with Travelodge's Sleepy Bear. Fly with the Ozark Go-Getter Bird, or, like Wally Bird, drink champagne while hitching a ride on the tail of a Western Airlines jet.

Mr. Happy Foot • 1954
McGregor Healthsocks hosiery
Detail of box

Little Miss Coppertone • 1956
Coppertone suntan lotion
Promotional store display

don't burn
use
PERTONE

Printed in Denmark   65599

Thrift Drug Pharmacist • c. 1960
Thrift Drug stores
Cover of matchbook

A Little Dab'll Do Ya • 1962
Brylcreem hair cream
Detail of promotional album jacket

Little Lulu • 1950
Kleenex tissues
Promotional store display

Col and Gate • 1957
Colgate shaving cream
Detail of magazine ad

ROMIKA
Elastik-Schuhe

Romika • c. 1968
Romika shoes
Detail of promotional store display

Mister Plus • 1953
The Mutual Broadcasting System
listenership promotion
Detail of promotional ink blotter

Johnny Mint • c. 1956
Squibb dental cream
Detail of magazine ad

Speedy • 1954
FTD flowers
Detail of magazine ad

REG. U. S. PAT. OFF.   REG. U. S. PAT. OFF.

Johnny Holiday • c. 1957
Holiday Inn hotels
Detail of hotel stationery

Go-Getter Bird • c. 1965
Ozark Air Lines
Detail of magazine ad

Lurchi • 1989
Salamander shoes
Detail of promotional booklet

Wool Council Lamb • 1957
The Wool Council
Detail of magazine ad

Kiwi • 1953
Kiwi boot polish and shoe cleaner
Detail of magazine ad

© CROWN ZELLERBACH CORP. 1974

Li'l Softee • 1974
Nice 'n Soft bathroom tissue
Promotional store display

Air-India Maharajah • 1956
Air-India International Airlines
Cover of in-flight menu

Woodsy Owl • 1973
Forest Service antipollution promotion
Promotional air freshener

Blackie • 1951
Cat's Paw rubber heels and soles
Detail of magazine ad

Sleepy Bear • 1954
Travelodge motels
Cover of matchbook

Thummer the Pig • 1960
The Los Angeles County Fair
Promotional decal

Hush Puppies Basset Hound • c. 1971
Hush Puppies shoes
Promotional store display

Jantzen Girl • 1946
Jantzen swimsuits
Detail of magazine ad

Harrah Genie • 1962
Harrah's Club casino and hotel
Promotional postcard

FREE
FUN BOOK

Miss Curity

coloring! stories!
games! puzzles!

and win a prize for having fun!

Boys! Girls! Enter Miss Curity's
4 big coloring contests

3241 PRIZES
$**1000** SAVINGS BOND
GRAND PRIZE

READ ABOUT IT INSIDE ▶

A GIFT TO
YOU FROM **Miss Curity**®

the first lady of first-aid

Copyright, 1952, the Kendall Company

Miss Curity • 1952
Curity first-aid bandages and tape
Detail of promotional booklet

Johnny-One-Note • 1945
Wurlitzer jukeboxes
Promotional sticker

Chico • c. 1957
Santa Fe Railway train lines
Detail of promotional notepad

Gertrude • 1946
Pocket Books paperback books
Detail of book cover

Good Sam • 1976
Good Sam Club RV owners' club
Promotional decal

Dashin' Dan • 1964
Long Island Rail Road commuter promotion
Promotional button

Cold Bug • 1966
Coricidin cold tablets
Promotional playing card

Speedy Alka-Seltzer • c. 1953
Alka-Seltzer effervescent tablets
Promotional store display

YOUR PLACE IN THE SUN IS

Tucson

IN FRIENDLY ARIZONA

Tucson Sun • 1959
Sunshine Climate Club tourism promotion
Detail of magazine ad

HAVE FUN IN THE SUN

LAS VEGAS NEVADA

Vegas Vic • c. 1955
Las Vegas tourism promotion
Promotional postcard

NEVADA CLUB

RENO

Nevada Club Man • 1960
Nevada Club casino
Detail of matchbook

Wally • 1960
Western Airlines
Detail of baggage label

Bucky Badger • 1957
Wisconsin tourism promotion
Detail of magazine ad

Varig Bird • c. 1960
Varig Brazilian Airlines
Detail of package header card

Sharpie • 1960
Gillette razor blades
Detail of promotional store display

Litterbug • c. 1960
Keep America Beautiful campaign
Detail of road map

Pal • 1946
Pal razor blades
Detail of magazine ad

Jockey • 1944
Jockey underwear
Detail of magazine ad

HIS Man • c. 1948
HIS toiletries
Detail of magazine ad

Major Zipper • 1942
Conmar zippers
Detail of magazine ad

UNDERNEATH IT ALL...A

Vassarette

Vassarette Girl • c. 1946
Vassarette hosiery and lingerie
Detail of box

Cappy • c. 1961
Capitol Records Junior Club
Detail of record sleeve

Bruno • c. 1970
HB cigarettes
Detail of promotional sticker

First • c. 1958
First National Bank of Meadville (PA)
Detail of coin-saver booklet

Crazy Eddie • 1975
Crazy Eddie audio stores
Detail of bag

Mets COLORING BOOK

50¢

© 1965 Metropolitan
Baseball Club, Inc.

"OH, WHAT A BEAUTIFUL DAY!"

Mr. Met • 1965
New York Mets major league baseball team
Cover of promotional coloring book

Newt • c. 1949
Apple Valley (CA) tourism promotion
Detail of company envelope

Count Rite • 1946
Count-Rite poker chips
Detail of magazine ad

Western Hotels Bellhop • 1952
Western Hotels
Detail of magazine ad

Tommy Trailways • 1953
Trailways bus lines
Detail of magazine ad

Esky • c. 1948
Esquire magazine
Promotional store display

ACKNOWLEDGMENTS

A very special thanks goes to "advertologist" and ephemera-hunter **Randy Jones** who generously contributed his many "Mr. Product" discoveries to this project.

Our gratitude to **Stephen Veltman**, **Roger Brittan**, **Ed Polish**, **Jeff Errick**, **Harry Devack**, **Gerry Rouff**, **Michelle Richards**, and **Dennis Weiss**. We'd also like to express our appreciation to **Alan Rapp**, our editor at Chronicle Books; to **Jodi Davis** for her thoughtful editorial direction and **Azi Rad** for her design expertise; and to **Jean Blomquist** and **Jeff Campbell**, for their thorough copyediting.

We'd like to recognize **McCrea Adams**, **Lincoln Diamant**, **John Flinn**, **Jim Hall**, **John Mendenhall**, **Hal Morgan**, **Jim Morton**, and **Ellen Havre Weis**, whose writings have inspired our own interest and fascination with "Mr. Product." Thanks also to **Chris Mullen** at the Visual Telling of Stories Web site, School of Design, University of Brighton, England.

Masud Husain would like to extend personal thanks to his beloved wife, **Jane Husain**, for her trust, inspiration, and insightful participation in the making of *Meet Mr. Product*.

Finally we wish to recognize and thank all the corporate sponsors, illustrators, and graphic designers of advertising characters, whose work appears in this book, and who have provided us with a glimpse of America's popular culture past.

His Royal Nibs...

His Royal Nibs • 1955
Nibroc paper towels
Detail of magazine ad

Tested Quality Doughnut Bakers • 1937
The Doughnut Corporation of America
Detail of magazine ad